# NEW SERIES!
## Asian Animals

**Reading Level: Grades K-1**
**Interest Level: Grades PreK-2**
Big, colorful photos and simple text explore these fascinating creatures. Simple maps show where each animal lives its amazing life.
Publisher: Capstone Press • Discount: 25% off list
Binding: Reinforced Library • Size: 11 x 9 • Pages: 24
Features: Full-Color Photographs, Websites, Read More, Glossary, Index

| | | |
|---|---|---|
| CAK469 | **ASIAN ANIMALS (Pebble Plus) (6 vols.)** | **101.94** |
| CA0329 | Bengal Tigers/Sirota, Spr 10 | 16.99 |
| CA9927 | Camels/Sirota, Spr 10 | 16.99 |
| CA0282 | Giant Pandas/Sirota, Spr 10 | 16.99 |
| CA029Y | King Cobras/Mattern, Spr 10 | 16.99 |
| CA0305 | Orangutans/Mattern, Spr 10 | 16.99 |
| CA0312 | Rhinoceroses/Mattern, Spr 10 | 16.99 |

## Asian Animals

# Orangutans

by Joanne Mattern

**Consulting Editor:** Gail Saunders-Smith, PhD

**Content Consultant:** Tanya Dewey, PhD
University of Michigan Museum of Zoology

CAPSTONE PRESS
a capstone imprint

Pebble Plus is published by Capstone Press,
151 Good Counsel Drive, P.O. Box 669, Mankato, Minnesota 56002.
www.capstonepress.com

092009
005618CGS10

 Books published by Capstone Press are manufactured with paper
containing at least 10 percent post-consumer waste.

*Library of Congress Cataloging-in-Publication Data*
Mattern, Joanne, 1963–
    Orangutans / by Joanne Mattern.
    p. cm. — (Pebble Plus. Asian animals)
    Includes bibliographical references and index.
    Summary: "Simple text and photographs present orangutans, how they look, where they live, and what they do" —
Provided by publisher.
    ISBN 978-1-4296-4030-5 (library binding)
    ISBN 978-1-4296-4848-6 (paperback)
    1. Orangutan — Juvenile literature. I. Title. II. Series.
QL737.P96M38 2010
599.88'3 — dc22
                                        2009028650

**Editorial Credits**

Katy Kudela, editor; Matt Bruning, designer; Svetlana Zhurkin, media researcher; Eric Manske, production specialist

**Photo Credits**

Alamy/Ben Oliver, 13; Alamy/Ben Queenborough, 21; iStockphoto/George Clerk, 19; Minden Pictures/Anup Shah, 5;
Peter Arnold/Biosphoto/Albert Visage, 7; Peter Arnold/Biosphoto/Cyril Ruoso, 11, 17; Peter Arnold/Wildlife, 15;
Shutterstock/Andy Z., cover; Shutterstock/capturefoto, 1; Shutterstock/Marcel Suliman, 9

## Note to Parents and Teachers

The Asian Animals series supports national science standards related to life science. This
book describes and illustrates orangutans. The images support early readers in understanding
the text. The repetition of words and phrases helps early readers learn new words. This book
also introduces early readers to subject-specific vocabulary words, which are defined in the
Glossary section. Early readers may need assistance to read some words and to use the Table of
Contents, Glossary, Read More, Internet Sites, and Index sections of the book.

# Table of Contents

# Living in Asia

Orangutans climb and swing through Asia's rain forests. As adults, these quiet apes live by themselves.

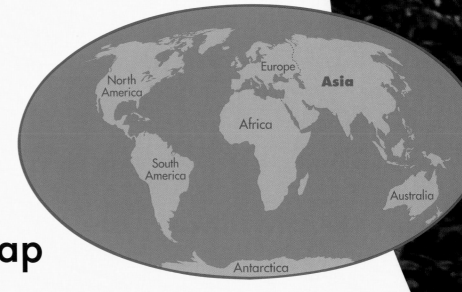

**World Map**

Orangutans live on the islands
of Borneo and Sumatra.
They build and sleep in
new nests each night.

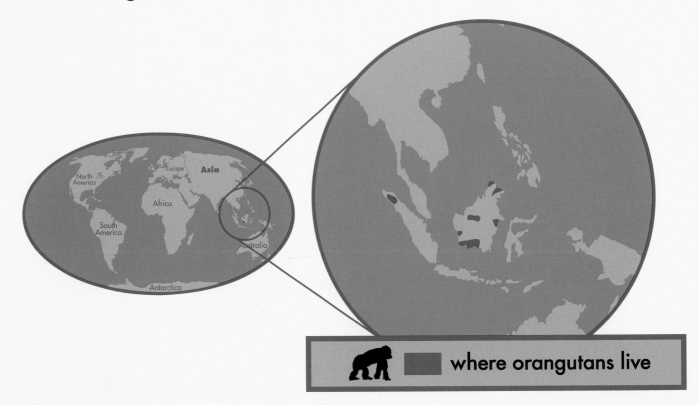

where orangutans live

# Up Close!

Orangutans have

thick, red-brown hair.

Hair covers their bodies

from head to toe.

Orangutans have long arms
to swing from tree to tree.
Their fingers and toes
grip branches and vines.

# Eating and Drinking

Orangutans munch on

fruits, nuts, and plants.

They also catch insects.

Orangutans use sticks

to dig insects from tree bark.

They use rocks to smash open

fruits and nuts.

Orangutans use their hands

to scoop water.

They also drink rainwater

that collects on leaves.

# Staying Safe

A mother orangutan
protects her baby.
She teaches her baby
to climb and find food.

Orangutans are endangered.

They have few places to live.

People passed laws

to protect orangutans

and their rain forest homes.

# Glossary

**ape** — a large animal related to a monkey but with no tail; chimpanzees, gorillas, and orangutans are kinds of apes.

**endangered** — in danger of dying out

**insect** — a small animal with a hard outer shell, six legs, three body sections, and two antennae; most insects have wings.

**law** — a rule made by the government that must be obeyed

**protect** — to keep safe

**rain forest** — a thick area of trees where rain falls almost every day

**vine** — a plant with a long stem that grows along the ground or climbs on trees, fences, or other supports

# Read More

**Armentrout, David, and Patricia Armentrout.**
*Orangutans.* Amazing Apes. Vero Beach, Fla.:
Rourke, 2008.

**Bredeson, Carmen.** *Orangutans Up Close.* Zoom
in on Animals! Berkeley Heights, N.J.: Enslow
Elementary, 2009.

**Underwood, Deborah.** *Watching Orangutans in Asia.*
Wild World. Chicago: Heinemann Library, 2006.

# Internet Sites

FactHound offers a safe, fun way to find Internet sites
related to this book. All of the sites on FactHound have
been researched by our staff.

Here's all you do:

Visit *www.facthound.com*

FactHound will fetch the best sites for you!

# Index

Word Count: 145
Grade: 1
Early-Intervention Level: 18